ADAM

GBOYEGA ODUBANJO

Adam

faber

First published in 2024
by Faber & Faber Ltd
The Bindery, 51 Hatton Garden
London EC1N 8HN

Typeset by Matthew Hollis
Printed in the UK by TJ Books Ltd, Padstow, Cornwall

A CIP record for this book is available from the British Library

ISBN 978-0-571-39040-3

MIX
Paper | Supporting
responsible forestry
FSC® C013056

Printed and bound in the UK on FSC® certified paper in line with our continuing
commitment to ethical business practices, sustainability and the environment.
For further information see faber.co.uk/environmental-policy

2 4 6 8 10 9 7 5 3

Contents

The Garden

it's us eyebrow slitted in the archives standing on the corner of here and there
    living dead as we could ever.
living like *free of air and full of ways to breathe.* dead like literally under thames vibing
    pretty darkly our shades still on because this the night beneath the night.
the life beneath the living. this the land where streets are paved with cousins.
we so inherent in this matter.
every man eating in every kitchen across the city so cross orbital.
this the last day of summer so we gather our uneaten yams and feed ourselves a liberty.
we dress up as each other we bear each other's names. someone says i knew your missus
    asks if bob's your uncle—no.
your uncle's adam. your mother—adam floating. your cousin—adam bleeding
    in the masquerade.
and still there's more arrivals—they're greeted with cups of river
    and given a week to change their names to adam.
we phone our loved ones. we tell the pregnant we've been reading the book
    and might have found the perfect name.
so what of tradition.
this is not our country this is not a country it's a burned CD and a tracklist
    we've written ourselves.

ADAM

On 21 September 2001, the torso of a black boy was discovered in the River Thames, near Tower Bridge in central London, clothed only in an orange pair of girls' shorts. Given the name 'Adam' by police officers, the unidentified boy was between four and eight years old. What comes next cannot without a story of water and offering. The sun shines and we gather because the river allows it. Na from clap dem dey enter dance. We enter with, and as, Adam.

Adam

first and foremost thank you to the coast because without the coast how do we
move from here to there how does the boy land in germany where an adult maybe
a woman buys a pair of orange shorts from woolworths thank you to those who
circumcise within the first few days meaning when i look at him at his self i know he
is from benin city i know from benin city they took him to hamburg thank you joyce
who he was handed over to and who brought him to london who after years said
this is ikpomwosa who a year later said actually this is patrick thank you joyce maybe
before it all happened you heard the boy coughing and gave him medicine maybe
the medicine put him to sleep maybe that's when thank you for doing what you were
told to do maybe telling them to make it quick telling them to start with his neck

thank you ceremony thank you tradition thank you river where he was
seen the last time the first thank you to the man who found him thank you orange
shorts for covering what shame he had thank you to the men in uniform who named
him adam because he was the first they'd seen because all of him was torso was body
was ribs because they knew adam was where knowing began

Breaking

looks like it'll be a rainy week ahead thank you   now the body
of an unidentified boy aged between four and seven
was   in the river for up to ten days before a passer by
noticed   african boy's stomach included extracts
of calabar   bean and flecks of gold expert at kew gardens
    says headless   limbless boy likely to be   nigerian
growing number have spread throughout the world   coming up
goat arrested for armed robbery prime minister's response breaking
male torso   boy five or six said to be somebody's
    son boy assigned most appropriate acceptable name
after long deliberation   thought to have been in river   ten days
appeal made to family of girls' shorts boy's   body
walking man who spotted adam to be offered counselling
suspicious thames river boy behaviour   should be reported
to authorities   in other news

The Lyric Adam

most commonly understood as the objective form of adam.
or—more simply—the speaking voice prompting the reader/witness/
    man who first sees the body in the thames to imagine adam—to try go
    beyond the page/thames and understand who adam is.
adam—the most appropriate and acceptable name—not deriving from
    ădāmâ.
not of soil or dust but water.
adam—from dam or damnation as in too much water or not enough.
adam as neither i nor you—still always us man and never *them man*.
newly invented adam overrepresented as the generic tosin-deji-and-wale
    ubiquitous human.
adam at the very centre—neither of paradise nor of earth—neither dead
    nor living but in fact actually found dead in the thames and actually
    the first man to live.

now adam emerges from the thames pointing to his stomach.
and because—as is recognised in the scientific literature—adam is what
    adam eats the stomach points to benin city.
benin city—however—cannot point to adam.
benin city knows only the actual boy—not anyone named adam.
adam—still emerging from the thames—thus finds not only a distance
    between himself and the reader/the passer-by as his body is lifted
    from the thames/the metropolitan police who would name him and
    claim to be his family but also a distance between himself and home.
but adam—emerged and still wet—has already moved on—however
    slightly—from the actual boy and is looking back from this distance—
    however minuscule—so that home is no longer so much home and
    the boy is no longer so much a boy.

oh wondrous and unsurpassable felicity of adam—to whom it is granted
to have and to be whatever.
adam—now—constitutes a unique authority.
not consigned to limits of perspective nor to the limits of intimate or
actual experience.
adam now sees the universality of adam.
everything of—and for—adam.
adam needs no subordinate or other.
adam finds always another adam in the adam—another river in the
river—another possession in what adam possesses—all the things and
all the beings implicated in adam's being.
adam—waking up in the cold light of adam—unable to see the woods
for adam.

because now emerging from the thames—after adam—comes every beast
of the field and every bird of the air and every man on the block to see
what adam would call them.
and adam says—you are now the wet of my wet—the adam of my adam.

the question remains.

i.

if adam—contrary to popular belief—doesn't fall but instead after the blood is
drained from the body adam is placed or dropped or thrown into the thames
and adam stays there for up to ten days before being seen where then is eden.

A Potted History of East

in the beginning.
it was a gush of us and we came from all over.
life was a bottle of nuts. one room and it was decent.
kept the cardamom in the cupboard above the bagels.
sixpence i'd make on an alright day. then independence came.
then war. then war. took me and my brothers.
the women built an estate for our ghosts. we manufactured fords
and drove them to the city gates demanding to be let in.
back then it was simple. sure we weren't squeaky clean
but we were easy. always punch up we said. no point
nicking some bloke's ped when the factory owner's balling
in his four-door. but then a sweet one makes you settle down a bit.
landlord gets the hump so you find another room.
store the polenta next to the cassava flour. get the jobs
where you can. someone's left their lamb leg in the pub again.
is this where eden is. where the sun rises.
developers calling it barcelona on thames now. council say
dagenham leo is alive and well. it's cold as chips
but the ice cream van is still going off and we're laughing.

we never unpacked.

so far east it's west to another man. no bells here.

still we move. almost back where we left now.

The Cow and the River

we wouldn't actually lay our hands on the cow.
i was never sure if cows could carry our sins
and even if they could i couldn't know how a cow
carrying all that sin would be received in whatever
world it ended up in. i saw my mate and we spoke
but i couldn't hear what they were saying because
of the singing as we all followed the cow through
the suburbs onto the tube and to the river. my friend
and i had always been close. always liked asking
each other questions that were hard to answer. like
what would you choose as your last meal. or how come
a scapegoat isn't actually a goat but a cow
or sometimes a boy. i wasn't near enough to the thames
to hear the cow itself but i could tell when it happened
because of the noise from everyone else.

A Story About Water

so there's a scorpion and a frog—they're trying to get across this river—the scorpion says to the frog take me—the frog says are you sure because if you sting me we'll both drown—the scorpion says of course i'm sure—so the frog takes the scorpion and the scorpion stings the frog and of course they both drown—wait actually it's two sisters—sorry—two sisters trying to get across this river—and the river says i'm gonna need something in order for you two to get across—the first sister says take my mangoes—the second sister says no you can't have my mangoes and she tries to go across and of course she drowns— besides the old man already told them don't go into the water—he said don't you know that that is how they took us—the younger sister probably forgot because the old man said a lot of things—he's the one who said two by two for forty days—sorry— different story—this old man said if you want the water to stop then plant a cross in the yard and sprinkle it with salt—but it didn't stop—whole time the sun and ocean are chilling on a bench—the ocean invites the sun to its house—the sun says how come you never visit my house—the ocean says i'm not sure if i should—the sun—of course you should— the ocean—are you sure there'll be enough room— the sun—of course i'm sure—so the ocean goes and fills up the whole living room—says are you sure— the sun says i'm sure—so the ocean fills the corridors stairs bedrooms the whole gaff—and so that's why the ocean is here and the sun all the way up there

Crown

head permed heavy because rain don't dare touch us.
on certain mornings you can hear it deep in conversation
with itself. i can't the rain says. for it is written that so long
as the oils of scorched earth red to the root and royal hold
the hair in place then it shall remain untouched. the world
must scab. the peacocks must shrivel into vultures
before the scalp is troubled. but it has been so long
the rain says since i have tasted. generations have come and
gone and still it holds. this immaculate empire without stray.

London Is the Place for Me

cool as a lord i landed in the mother
blitzed and tipsy on the foreign extra
brought the pot to boiling and i melted
said every man come with because

london is the place for me
london is the place to be

cruising and reclining in old albion
trafficating through the big city
everything copacetic everything
the expensivest everything luxury
everything on credit highlife lovely
every ting na double double everything

london na be de place for me
where i dey chop money i dey
chop corn london na be de place

on a tour de blighty
where here the gist is
i wake the sun
the water drinks me

london is a bit of me
london is the place for me

ii.

if adam is naked and someone owns a pair of orange shorts from woolworths and covers adam what then is shame.

Shorts Weather

man went park. this day hot as feast. adam'd himself. took two ribs
and belly skin. lick tune and stretch them tight as sticks and
drum. it was good like scrunch your face like this that shame.
people come with coin. with ooh lah lahs. say good good.
say wonderful good. now give us hip. want neck. want nyash.
fat from back of head that folds. want crook of you. the sex still in it.
behind the knee where hand fits so. fingered gum. flab of ear. damp
crease. damn sure it's music there.

Pigeon

the same the same   their purr
purr our brap brap   we used to be doves
one pigeon says to the other
out of bed into each flush morning
red green olives for brekky   garveyism
in the city weeds blood on the flag
of the federal republic
    or maybe it was all butt ends
of meat chicken change
bopping heads to our every survival
but that's enough with history
come we flock just paint the town
shit on monuments   the mayor
try phase us out still i coo coo
perched on the lifting
while you cool cool
    sermoning to all those tuned in
to the rooftops and the underground

Function

just a little spot we had and it was our world
top notch residents we were   never did a madness
didn't once bowl in lathered and piss in the potpourri
sure we enjoyed   when the barman came out from under the bed
and the mccoys were on the house   pennies in the jukebox
last entry at two and then they locked us in

or did we lock ourselves in
everyone clapping   the children picking money off the ground
putting it in black bags for the celebrants   elders putting up flags
because they said we couldn't paint the walls breaking clocks
when they said we had fifteen minutes left in the hall
we saw smoke   realised it was lit

was nang was heavy was bad was sick
the roof the roof on fire   water wasted on the drunk
blues and twos roused and wooing
a thousand soldiers at the door looking for their bit
of slap and tickle   mothers jumping out of windows
backs breaking in the dance   no doctors in the room

They Adam

wake up vomiting
cowries into
their hands like
some childdead
bird
pretending to feed
except this is
one of those
pleasant sousings
you hear about
and here they
come with a
warm cup of
afternoon
and they're like
hope you're proud
the a-roads
are soaked
your trousers
are in the wash
but it is good
as are the actual
birds in their
units feeding
and traditional
besides the city
is hanging
up to dry and
they content
simply to flow

no ancestry
other than the
spill of them
one squiffy fatberg
whole and
messy in
their effluvia
the swig of their
backwash the
taste of last
night's tonic
on them they
forecasting
spit hands
reaching for
their refusal
to be something
sliding out
plentiful as
that first glass
of tap
that they
all claimed
contaminated

Rewilding

it was the rainy season so it rained. the old man snored. these times the river
like a boy was either missing or was everywhere you looked. in the east it was
everywhere because they had convinced themselves it didn't exist. newbuilds
and roundabouts existed. the river was just a story they thought. so they planned
their journeys to the minute not knowing where they had come from. but it
rained so there was rain and because the people had forgotten the river had to
retell its story. it said before anything there was water and there was water. on
one side you. on the other side you. the people mistook this for a riddle. each
claiming a side for themselves. the river welcoming the people in their entirety.
taking in them the clothes on their backs all that they clung to.

Makoko Adam

like a tourist i navigate you no baseline data no big man
to bless my coming just a bottle of gin and a prayer
your insults so fitting my city smell my gerrymandering
all barracuda through your floating settlement you so non
communicable me so dredging your lagoon waiting
for the high tide to tell me what will last what won't
can't you translate for me talk back just this once

iii.

if adam is naked but—having had the flesh around the limbs and neck cut down to the bone then slashed with a single blow—has no way of seeing or touching said nakedness on what day does adam acquire the knowledge of good and evil and surely die.

Genesis

then god said   let me make man in my image
man in my likeness   man like me
man like light and man like dark
let man nyam and chop whatever   be good
    god said   give man arm to skank   leg to shake
tongue and chest to speak with
give man cash to spray   put man's face on it
   said give man sea and sky and trees
and zones one to six on the oyster so man can see it
               now man said   rah   swear down
                 man said   show me

* * *

You: The Many Adams of Adam

you were a boy.   i was a boy.
you came from benin city.   my dad would
drive me to school in the mornings.
you were taken to hamburg then london.   i went to new york once
i remember it like it was yesterday.
by the time you arrived in london the leaves
were already browning the thames coming
up to its last blue days.   new york was nice
they had their own river i got told not to throw
things in it because i didn't know where
it could end up.   you didn't know where you
would end up.   did your favourite river look better
or worse in the summer.   i wish i'd gotten close enough
to touch it.   did you ever swim in it or maybe float.

you were a boy

i was a boy

but now because the sun

is so much in our faces

when i look at you standing on the

second floor balcony   me in the grounded

belly of this estate shielding

the glare from my eyes   you become

a body of light   faint like tomorrow

today you could be cousin lover

bosom of abe   all i hope is that

in my squint you don't see me screwing

i'm just fleshing you out   praying

you don't see a problem in me

and now i'm on the mezzanine
the light all on you and when you say top five dead
or alive i believe it i saw the come up you wouldn't
know this but we're around the same age my
aunty worked at your school i had my phone to
the telly it was me first thing on release day through
the door past the pick 'n' mix ten quid for the album
i saved up and as soon as i saw the face on the cover
the little boy i knew it was you the struggle in those
eyes man i know a real one when i see one couldn't be
no one else i knew your name before you had a name
i learnt all of your bars even the freestyles the leaks test me

yo   you should've seen yourself
last night   you were   head gone
swede done in   up to the neck
in tipple   when i say legless i mean
actually   top heavy   you forgot your name
when the bouncer asked
you two sheets with
a skin full   all mops and brooms drunk as a don
fallen from grace you

everyone says we raised each other
child parents role modelling innocence
we each proud of our firstborn the boy leading
the boy   this explains why i don't know
whose idea it was or where the chicken came from
i'm told that when we were done it lay twitching at the bottom
of a bucket covered in leaves and what we thought seasoning
that the idea of sacrifice still confused us both
presenting our gift to who we thought gods our parents
only grateful that in search for offering
we hadn't thought to call on ourselves

you call and i'm there   my man from day
everyone always talking about how you allegedly
did this did that but no one knows you like i do
the way when we hug you hold your fist to my heart
and you keep it   my man with the yellow eyes
and the moschino eating plantain straight out the oil
as uncles prostrate   my man with the bootcuts
and the barrel chest you like your prune juice with ice and i oblige
everyone always looking for my man
but i never worry   you're everywhere at all times
and at home between the hours of seven and seven
come we go wherever i'll play the tunes on the drive
and when we get to the coast you'll dive right in
and tell me i'll be fine

                    or   i'm not there
              and as much as none of this happen
        none of it could   because centuries ago the wind
          carried whoever it was that would become you
              not to benin city but to dakar to abidjan
       instead of plantain you say alloco instead of london
              paris on est la hein i don't know
          help me   in how many rivers are there boys
                washing their hair and swimming
              and seeing themselves for the first time
           resting their eyes and are they not the same
            waters if i keep going will i not eventually
  find you on a bank waiting your toes smoothing the ripples
            your hand out bonjour   je m'apelle

it's been a hot minute since we've seen you.
not much has changed around here. everyone
still asks of you. they finally repainted the
football cage. remember whatshisname who
always wore the white air forces when we
played and then punched that kid in the mouth
because he stepped on them. punched him so hard
that summer only lasted two weeks that year.
well everyone started calling him two step
after that because you always stay two steps
back when you're near him. they even started calling
his son little two step. two step hates it.
he tells people who don't know
that he got the name because of the way he dances.
tells his son just how quickly you can lose yourself.

do you remember the mannequins
how you swore to me that they were real
people   steady in their lifelessness
and from a distance i believed you
thinking what it must be like to be so image
and still
i remember you
would disappear and the next thing i would see
was your face above a parapet of body
playing whoever you wanted to be that day

it's been long enough i can say
we fully tried to be you   everytime
we got stopped it was your name we used
even the papers confused us   for the mug
of you   of course we took it too far   it was you
applying for the jobs and providing the reference
the emergency contact   wouldn't be no us
without   every new face i see could be yours
a gang of you   for us you are
to us you return   everyday the newest

✱ ✱ ✱

Genesis

and on the second day nothing.
and on the third day nothing. and
on the fourth the fifth the sixth
seventh nothing because adam
already was.

hello hello to i'm only taking what was mine already bossman. i'm gonna look right at the camera when i take what was mine to have and sell if i need to. hello hello to he gave me a key to the city. i've just gone and made copies given one to my bredrin his bredrin. in the beginning he said man in my likeness in my image man like me. like me. he said in the name of my man and my man let man dry hump on the riverbed if he's got nowhere else to go and the mood is agreeable. don't worry we'll change the sheets when we're done we'll air out the firmament. he said give man sea and sky so if every cloud has a silver chain around its neck we'll be having that too. he said let man fix the sun to his incisors if it shines right. hello hello to rah. all of this for man. hello to show me.

The Drums Sing of Adam

the place the child was found
                                is where the gods stay
                we don't fish or gather there
        we are all very shocked
                boys they are stubborn
            it is not clear how the child
                    got past the authorities
        a deer that is bound to die
will mistake a warning for a chorus
                    the boy was smart
        and that is why it took us
                        so long to find him
                a water insect that dances
        on the surface surely has its
                    musicians located on the riverbed
        there will be nothing that can
                        tell a large group of people
                        what do with their necks in this song

Should You Return

just be sending the money and the land will be here waiting for you
the price the builder gave you is not a serious price unless you don't want joy
if you don't like the way the sun shines in the morning we can bring you a new one
the local guys will say you should pay tax but we can sort that one out
you want everything included school hospital transport we can build
there's nothing like government policeman no dey for centre everything we can do
if anyone should try to rob you believe me the smoke will clear before you hear sound
if you want the house to be a cure a meal an ocean we can manage
there is space for you your children their children their concubines their ghosts
when you are coming let us know the diesel will be in the generator
the guinness will be cooking the family you don't know they will come and eat
and only when they are full will they remember that the rain has finished

Bronze Adam of Benin

if walking through your home as the day becomes itself
you find the bed of your only son empty do not panic.
decline all media requests. ignore the authorities
for they cannot help and there is work to be done.
you have prepared exactly for this. the longer
you take to make a mould of your son the harder
it will become to remember him. to ensure that the head
of your son is lifelike close your eyes as you meld it.
think of how his nostrils flared as he grinned
in the face of your worry. now cream the mask
in spit and clay. swaddle it firm to your chest
just as you would an actual boy. pour molten bronze directly
onto your chest and let it flow into the gap of your cradle.
rest so you wake to your son's burnished eyes free from tears or want.
people will have by now heard of your work
and will travel to bear witness. do not allow visitors.
instead make an altar for your son and on days
when his laugh echoes inside you go to the altar
and wear your son and tell yourself that you are right there.

To the High Commissioner

i'm gagging to live but forgetting how to
do so with the required spite. i trust you have
received my letters. when will it be my turn
to inflict the generational trauma. the ideas
i have. in every room another war
to kiss and baby to condemn. i'm too late.
on my behalf please let everyone know
that i won't be parting with any money.
i don't care whose round it is. no applications
are currently being accepted. this is the sweet spot. besides
london is finished. zip up the river. we've outsourced the dying.
there are enough curses on my name that no one need
ever get close enough to hurt me. tell everyone
that there's no point them having children
because here we've already struck bronze
and life isn't half as good if everyone gets one.

Against Resting in Peace

there you go telling me what to do still like i ain't been here listening i washed
my ass took my vitamin d i voted phoned my mum twice a week bought my man
outside the station hot drinks i deleted social media turned off the tv i didn't just
read the headline i didn't say anything i knew it would harm my defence i didn't
go to bed upset i didn't cross the picket line didn't walk under ladders i texted
you when i got home i kept my hands where you could see them i supported
independent bookshops dealers the youth i drank fourteen units of alcohol a
week eight glasses of water a day one glass of warm milk before bed i fucking
i didn't expect you to say it back i just said it because i meant it at the time
honestly i'm okay now i'm six feet one point eight two metres two yards deep
and you still want me to listen peace you say

Dip

pastor wet me down. please today undo me.
when i was younger i got pulled bawling from the tub.
i would soak till i was pruned and let the
    lukewarm stew me.
only a matter of time before the lights went out and
    while the generator started up i'd look upon a dark
    blue me.
all this time it felt like i'd been swimming in a drum till
    the lid came off and i was borned a new me.
and it was on this day that it was said that this world
    belongs to me.
and i dare any man come here and try slew me.
promise that when i'm gone
    you won't let anyone try say they knew me.
the only place of rest will be where i was made
    and came to know myself so please on that day
    subsume me.

.

The Boy Who Became a River

the river had of course known many people some of them surely boys
but it had learned not to get too attached. so when one day the river
found itself by the boy neither expected much. the boy shocked to see
what could so easily be himself in the river bent to greet it. the river
who had forgotten what it was like to be looked at stepped towards the boy.
   the boy the river.
their body passing through the city under bridges. jumping over barriers.

Àbíkú Adam

we called him the beginning. we begged that he stay but
he didn't hear word. instead he came and went for the first
and repeated time and when he returned he was two halves
of a gourd longing to flesh. each time the cuts were the surgical same.
there are some who claim they saw him walk on water some
who swear he floated. sometime after the war he arrived
one by one into the homes of the victors playing on a
thumb piano singing his miserable life how lonely it was
until one day in the market he saw one miserable as he
and followed him into a silk tree where were gathered
children—for he too was a child—all with his exact scars
and foibles besides themselves trading deaths like marbles.

Arrangements

it goes like this
one two three everybody blow your trumpets
(nananananananana) that's it
now percussion from the left echoing against the half-hollow of the coffin
                                        damp condolence in your face
    wet lip of liturgy bottled malt on teeth one bucket one life goes the song

cut to outside everybody and their narrative in the procession
volume up to why not
                            horns blasting on arrival
let's be having you the palm oil suckers local fetishists straight gin sippers
    security at the door checking diacritics

this is the chorus   this is the bridge now get over it
that's the soul train coming   deities bopping through one by one with their claim to spirit
        which god you got your money on
        which mob you calling when you got mourning on your mind

for the outro some imagination
here the family   here we glance the restful face   here limbs

                                        anyone older than the dead
                                        to pay respects and leave

                        keys to close as family fades to one continuous ayy
a diminuendo of children remain to bury
they the true mourners   their faces we sing ourselves to sleep with

Traffic

it's bodies in all
their profit
changing hands
a prayer for a
kidney heart full
of money imported
roses spilling from
pockets no change
for a tenner everything
for sale ballad and
symphony traffic
conductor centre stage
giving it the head
shoulders knees
it's us rubbernecking
london bridge
is down again
a boy sent off
for a song again
driver at the ten
and two as if we
haven't already
donned the toga of
a dying god
you drive better
with the spirit in you
without a skeleton
in your backseat
how long can we
stay here in this

unmoving riddle
really it's until
the AC packs up
or the sacrificial
cows go home
the children are
released from the
forest someone finally
asks do you know
these people are you okay

Mama Adam

the large rock the size   of what is good   it fell   from the hills and just
missed the playground   it didn't hurt the children   so we called it mother
the boy didn't he was the only one who didn't instead   the boy he called out to his
mother as the rock rolled towards past   the playground and took to the water
like on another day a boy might   and everyone turned   to the boy
who called mother because   he said it and because now   mother was
in the water everyone said where   this mother   and nothing happened the rock
floated away   no one had a mother but the boy
now in their shock   turned to the boy   they called mother

A Story Without Water

no such thing as death by water

                          all pangaea all close enough

to rub

       friction full impossible for anybody to have been captured

entering the water

             sweet thames

a bullshit song a quick dip a fallacy   here

is no water no enemy

                   no attempt at rescue it was summer so the family

went for a chill stroll at the bottom of the pool the grass was actually brown

breaking   a man drags his ark towards salvation everyone laughs

the glass is completely empty the glass is redundant what could it hold

no wine because boy

             nothing to turn into wine there has never been a party

a baptism a wake nobody celebrates everybody is born in sin

                        and stays there

no here no there none undone instead of dying just decide not to

no reason to explain there is nothing of ourselves we ever need to clean

Isọmọlórúkọ

àkàndé
igbókọyí
béjídé
àmọ̀kẹ́
ọláídé
àbíkú
yétúndé
babátúndé
kòkúmọ́
ọmọ́tánwá
ọmọ́bọ̀wálé
ọmọ́dilé
dúró
orúkọtán
kòsókó
dúrójaiyé
dúrósinmí
àkànjí
èjíwùmí
ọmọ́nìtàn

first born
the one who the forest rejected
the one that comes with rain
loving stroke
wealth rolled in
one who dies and dies again
the mother has returned
the father has returned
do not die again
the child we searched for
the child who returned home
the child who became the home
wait
all the names have been exhausted
there is nothing left to dig a grave
wait and enjoy life
wait and bury me
your touch is life
your gapped teeth please me
the story is yours

Reload

remembering the boy
who was named adam
piece by actual piece re
membering him first
his legs then his arms neck
his head name the river
remembered into the channel
the channel into the ocean
the flood remembered in
to the pocket of the gods
the prodigal into the home
the dead remembered out
of their finest suits into
our fresh wagwans and our
thickest stouts our individual
theres into a single here

Adam's Law

from the twenty-first day of september two thousand and one
    every person born within the ague   shall be a citizen   any person who was
        a subject or alien
if he is of excellent character
    has sufficient knowledge of one or two idiolects   shall become a happy man
    state brigadish shall have no responsibility thereof
for this world go start   subject to the provisions
    the underground wahala
every person born within this geographical expression   infrastructural el dorado
    we all sing together   freely and sardonically and lugubriously   reh teh teh
    we all sing
the teacher schoolgirl schoolboy
let's get down in the cankerous tribalism   who be teacher in the malodorous saga
        cum gargantuan gaga
    we all mishmash
me and you no need dey for same category
the qualifications of citizenship therefore are
    it is to be obtained by means of fraud
    we to be compos mentis reh teh teh
    political hallelujah boys
and let us think say   for the reference therein   to the veritable bugaboo
    the english language must be pooh pooh-ed quod erat demonstrandum
        reh teh teh
let's wallow in the bluest dye   conceal all material fact
every person recognised in this interpose this democracy this demonstration
        of craze this economic
quagmire this cataleptic   shall on this date

* * *

Man

no manners always manic in the manor where manaman
demand dismantling mandatory unmanning
there's too many man too many many—
remand the policeman taxman informants
got the hangman on pager
understand that it's us man and it's them man
and when i say us man i proper mean all of us
man's adamant about semantics bildungsroman not a
    romance
go mano-a-mano with the badman
the mannish winner takes mansion and manilla
    but if man know you then it's just mandem innit
come nyam manna at the mangrove we the menace and
    the manager singing mantra till the morning come
in the name of my man and my man somebody say amen

* * *

Editorial Note

Before Gboyega Odubanjo passed away in the summer of 2023, he had exchanged three full-length drafts of *Adam* with his editor at Faber & Faber, and while he would likely have engaged in further revision, the typescript he had produced by that time had reached a state of near finality. The text of this edition reflects the author's last intentions as shared with his publisher, and has been posthumously supervised by this editorial panel on behalf of his family.

We wish to thank the editors of the following journals and broadcasts in which some of these poems have appeared: *bath magg, Faber Poetry Podcast, Five Dials, INQUE, New Yorker, Poetry, Poetry Ireland Review, Poetry Please, Poetry Review, Tangerine, TANK* and *Wasafiri*. In addition, we would like to offer our personal thanks to Joe Carrick-Varty, Hamish Ironside and Rose Olufuwa, who aided us in our textual work, and to Amy Acre, Rachael Allen, Anthony Anaxagorou, Raymond Antrobus and Jake Wild Hall, who helped in the documentation and publication of a number of these poems.

Nothing can replace a beloved friend, brother and son, but we hope that this volume constitutes a production in which the author would have found satisfaction and joy. It has been a privilege to help it complete its journey into print.

SURESH ARIARATNAM
VICTORIA ADUKWEI BULLEY
TICE CIN
MATTHEW HOLLIS

Family Note

As Gboyega Odubanjo's family, we extend our deepest gratitude to his close friends, esteemed colleagues and the dedicated team at Faber. Your unwavering support and collaborative spirit have been instrumental in bringing the final details of Gboyega's work to fruition. Your commitment not only honours his memory but also ensures his voice continues to resonate within the literary world and beyond.

We would also like to express our heartfelt thanks to the broader community of readers, poets and scholars whose engagement with his poetry has been a source of comfort and pride for us, illuminating the paths his words have travelled and the lives they have touched.

It is our hope that Gboyega's spirit of mentorship, creativity and exploration will live on, inspiring future generations to pursue their passions with courage and authenticity.

Love,

THE ODUBANJO FAMILY